Beethoven
Symphonies No. 1 & 2
for Solo Piano

Beethoven Symphonies No. 1 & 2 for Solo Piano

Copyright © 2025 by John Montroll. All rights reserved.
No part of this publication may be copied or reproduced by any
means without the express written permission of the author.

ISBN-13: 979-8-3484-9272-4

Antroll Publishing Company

Beethoven Symphonies No. 1 & 2 for Solo Piano

Transcribed by John Montroll

Antroll Publishing Company

Introduction

The first two symphonies by Beethoven are lively and began to challenge the construct of the symphonic form from the classical period. While symphonies from the classical period were centered around the strings, Beethoven used the woodwinds, horns and percussion to a greater effect.

I enjoy playing these symphonies on the piano. Liszt transcribed the Beethoven symphonies as grand works, but I found them too difficult to play. Checking Beethoven's score, the arrangements were needlessly complex. Other arrangements were too thin. As I enjoy transcribing orchestra works for piano, I set out to do so for the Beethoven symphonies.

When transcribing, my intent is to be playable as a Beethoven piano sonata, be faithful to Beethoven, and create a symphonic sound.

If you enjoy performing and making videos, I would be happy if you post them on Youtube. Or we can see if anyone else has done so.

I hope you enjoy the Beethoven symphonies on piano.

John Montroll

www.johnmontroll.com

Contents

        Beethoven Symphony No. 1, Opus 21

8   1st Movement

21   2nd Movement

27   3rd Movement

31   4th Movement

        Beethoven Symphony No. 2, Opus 36

40   1st Movement

60   2nd Movement

71   3rd Movement

75   4th Movement

Symphony No. 1

Beethoven premiered his first symphony on April 2, 1800 at the Burgtheater in Vienna. Mozart and Haydn works were performed and most likely Beethoven himself performed one of his early piano concertos. Haydn's last symphony was performed five years prior and Mozart's last (the Jupiter Symphony) was twelve years prior.

The symphony was well established by Mozart and Haydn, from the classical period. At the time, the symphony was musically complex and audiences expected a certain style. Beethoven wrote his first symphony using many of the standards from the classical period but added his own qualities. This includes greater use of the horns, woodwinds, and percussion. He placed a few musical jokes throughout. His new approach began at the dawn of a new century.

1st Movement: Adagio molto – Allegro con brio.

Written in sonata form, Beethoven opens the symphony with a slow introduction where he playfully tries to find the right key. He goes through a few different keys until concluding with C major. The exposition takes off with energy and excitement. The development section is filled with unusual key changes. A triumphant coda ends the first movement.

2nd Movement: Andante cantabile con moto.

Beginning with the violins playing a melody, more instruments join in as the melody is repeated in a fugue-like fashion. The use of woodwinds and tympani throughout the movement brought new life into the construct of a symphony that previously relied more heavily on the strings.

3rd Movement: Menuetto: Allegro molto e vivace.

This lively movement is played so quickly, it is more of a scherzo than a minuet. While in the key of C major, it soon shifts to D flat major, presenting unusual ideas at that time.

4th Movement: Adagio – Allegro molto e vivace.

As the first movement began with a musical joke, in finding the key, the fourth begins with a musical joke as the violins play a series of scales, each starting over while adding another note, leading to the exposition. Written in sonata form, the exposition is lively. The coda ends triumphantly with the horns and scales. Throughout the symphony, many musical ideas that Beethoven presented were revolutionary.

Symphony No. 2

Beethoven's Symphony No. 2 was premiered at the Theater an der Wien on April 5, 1803. Beethoven conducted this along with his Symphony No. 1, Piano Concerto No. 3 and other works. While still following Haydn's symphonic approach, Beethoven added many new elements.

1st Movement: Adagio molto – Allegro con brio

The first movement in sonata form begins with a long introduction. Symphony No. 1 has a short introduction, as he is making jokes wondering what key it will be in. For No. 2, it is a long and serious introduction. Once the exposition appears, the music is fun, playful, energetic and majestic.

2nd Movement: Larghetto.

The second movement is as peaceful and serene as could be. It includes some drama as if there are thunderstorms, but most is relaxing. I could even see how this would lead to the second movement of the Pastoral (6th symphony).

3rd Movement: Scherzo.

The scherzo and trio of the third movement is clever and playful. It contrasts with the minuets from the Haydn symphonies. The oboe and bassoon play important parts.

4th Movement: Allegro molto.

The fourth movement is also playful and energetic. It is considered to be full of musical jokes that only Beethoven could achieve. The long coda has its own development section that adds to the many surprises of the entire work.

There is a transcription of this symphony, as a trio for piano, violin and cello. Sources show it was written by Beethoven's pupil Ferdinand Ries and heavily overlooked by Beethoven, so it is as close to the orchestra score as can be. It appears to be the only transcription of the symphonies which involves Beethoven himself.

I used this transcription along with the full orchestra score for my arrangement. I was fascinated to see how Beethoven would manage his own work: The piano trio added notes, thicker chords, octave changes, (and omitted parts) as compared to the orchestra score, yet has a powerful sound, adds simplicity to the piano, while maintaining a symphonic quality. There were several passages where I had to choose between the orchestra score, or his piano trio arrangement. Should I pick Beethoven, or... Beethoven? Hence, this piano transcription might as well be by: Beethoven/Beethoven/Montroll.

Symphony No. 1 Opus 21

L. van Beethoven
Piano transcription by John Montroll

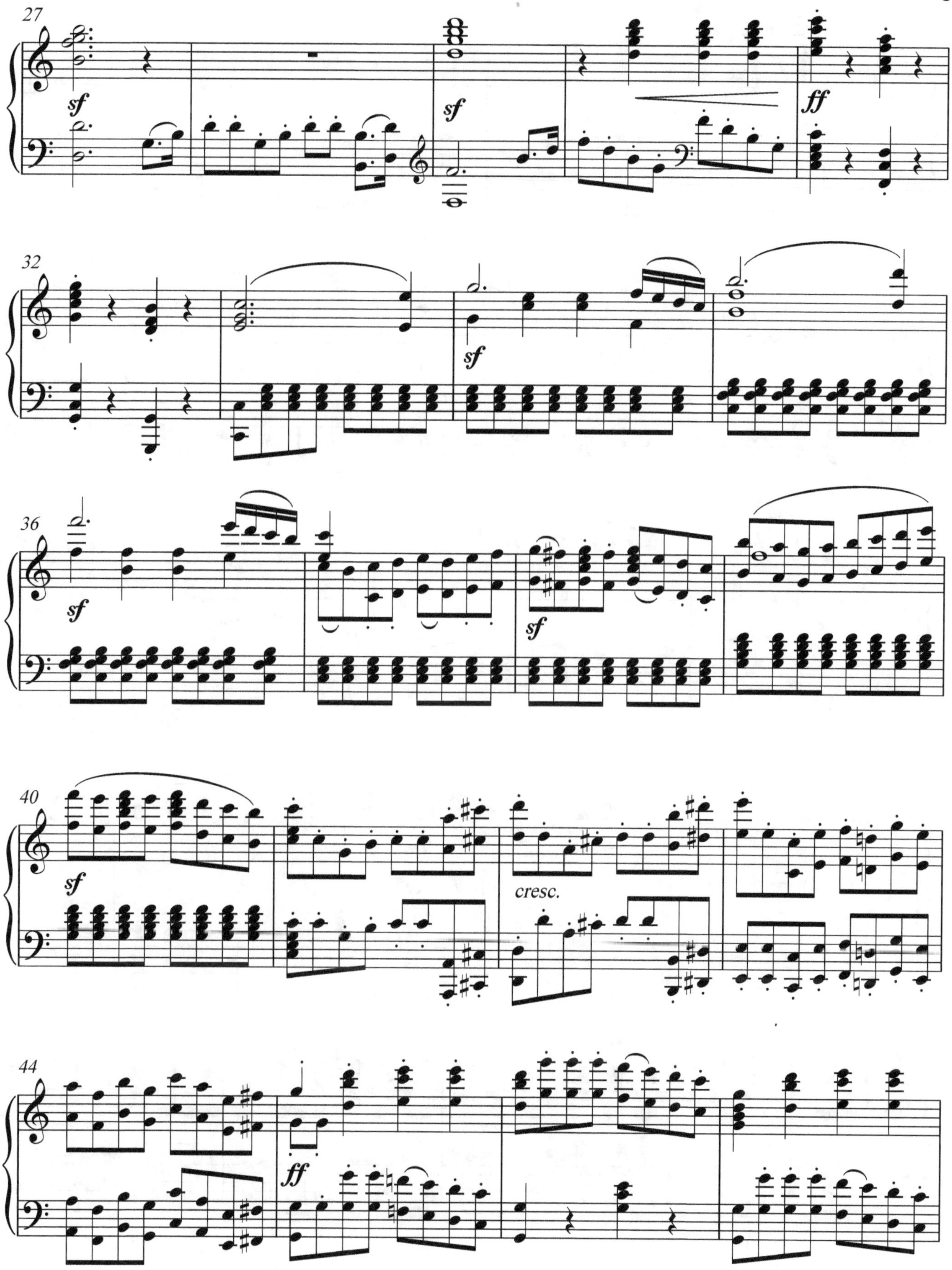
27
sf
sf
ff
32
sf
36
sf
sf
40
sf
cresc.
44
ff

II

EXPOSITION

Andante cantabile con moto ♪ = 120

III

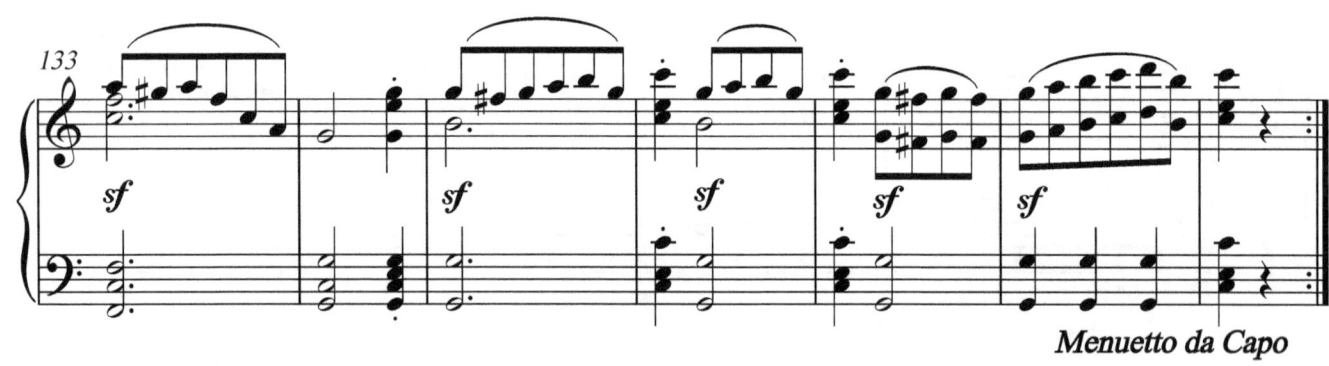

Menuetto da Capo

IV

Symphony No. 2 Opus 36

INTRODUCTION
Adagio molto ♪ = 84

I

L. van Beethoven
Piano transcription by John Montroll

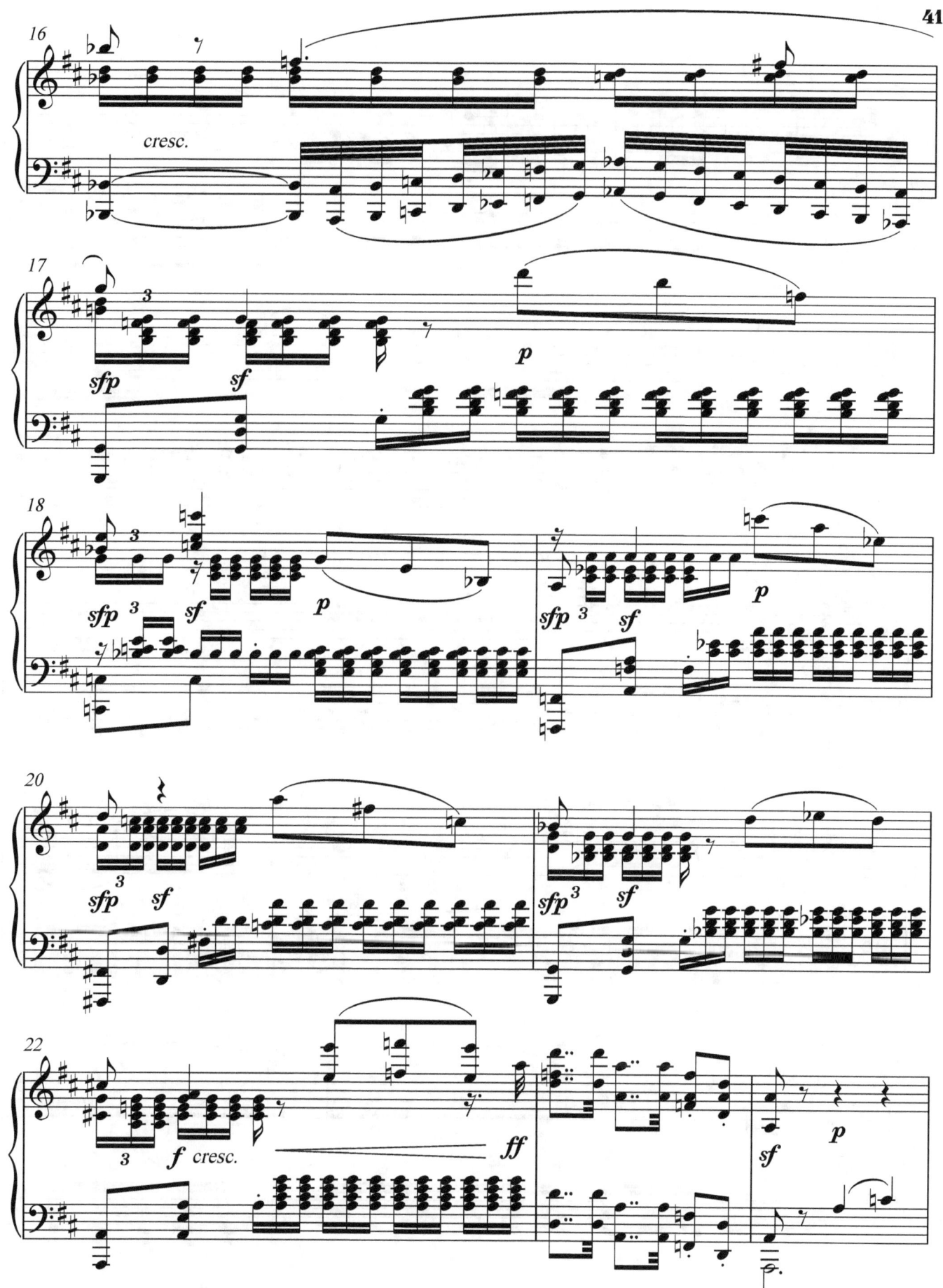

EXPOSITION
Allegro con brio ♩= 100

II

64

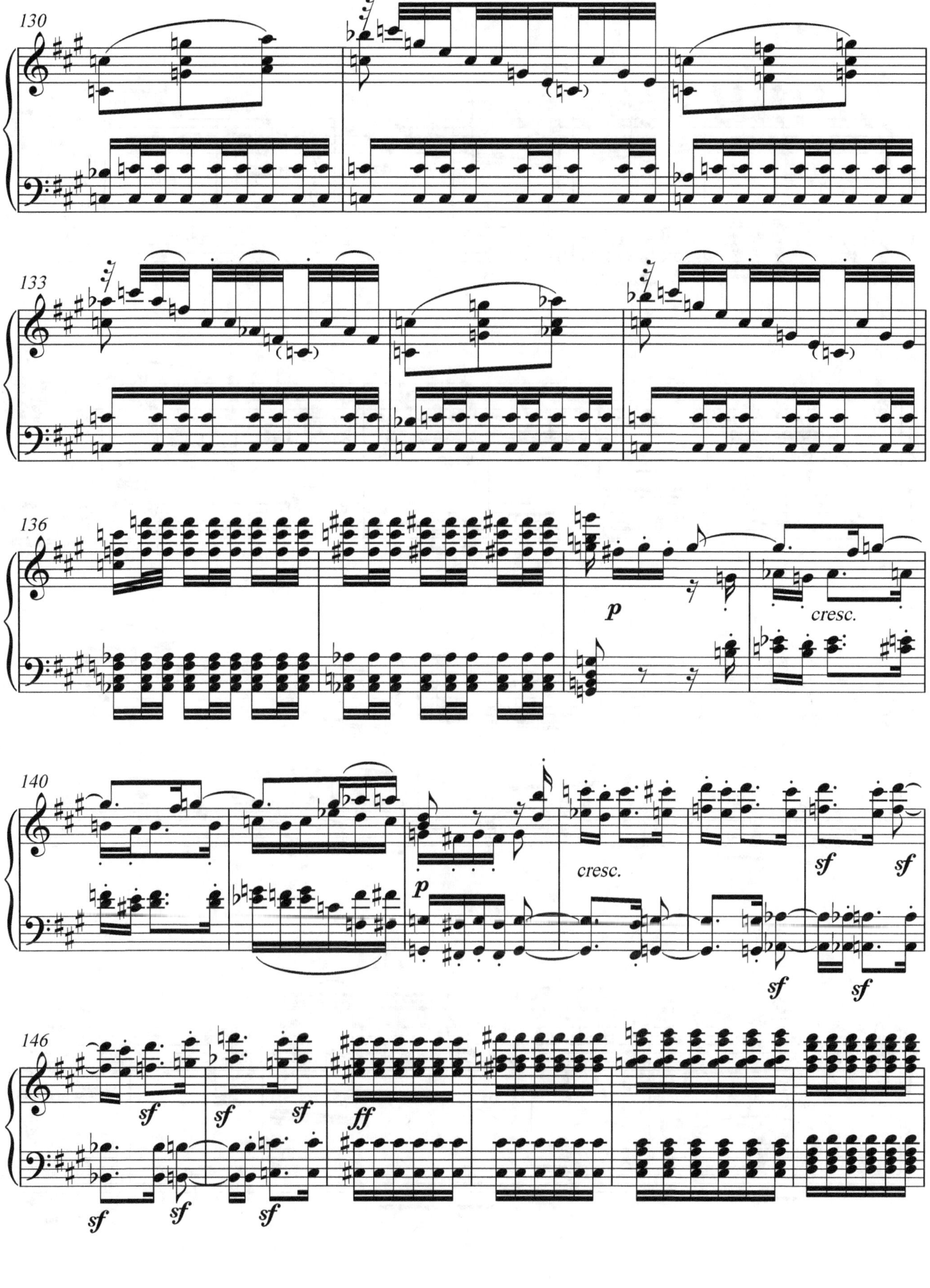
130
133
136
p
cresc.
140
p
cresc.
sf
sf
sf
sf
146
sf
sf
sf
ff
sf
sf
sf

RECAPITULATION

III

72

Scherzo da Capo

IV